MUST COME DOWN

These parachutists hope to land in one of the fields below. up to you to direct them into the right field based on the answer to each problem.

24 + 13

33 + 23

19 - 3

25 + 21

12 + 26

45 - 24

57 - 25

57 + 22

28 - 13

49 - 36

ODD

EVEN

Answer on page 48

COWBOY CASH

*H*owdy, pardners! Welcome to the 1880s. Before you can ride out, you've got to pick up some clothing and supplies. We've given you the money to pay for each item at

Illustration: Rick Geary

Answer on page 48

the price it would have cost in the 1880s. It's up to you to count the money and fill in each price tag. When you're done, add up all the price tags to find the grand total.

SHE LOVES ME

All the numbers on the daisy petals equal the sum at the center— all the numbers except one, that is. Can you pick off a single extra petal from each flower?

Hint on page 46

6   *MATHMANIA*

Answer on page 48

Illustration: Don Robison

TALLEST OF ALL

Gee whiz, we don't know which giraffe is the tallest. You can help by converting the sizes into the greatest number of feet and inches.

Hint on page 46

Ally
222 inches

Bozz
13 feet 56 inches

Cosmo
8 feet 102 inches

Denali
1 foot 184 inches

Elsa
5 feet 164 inches

Answer on page 48

Illustration: David Helton

BUBBLE BUDDIES

Billy's blowing big bubbles! But you shouldn't have any problem filling in the bubbles with the right math symbols. All you need to figure out is how the first two numbers equal the number on the right.

A. 5 + 9 = 14

B. 7 16 23

C. 21 7 3

D. 27 3 9

E. 33 11 22

F. 3 4 12

G. 28 4 24

Illustration: R. Michael Palan

8

Always start with the bubble on the left when working the problem. Write the math symbol in the small bubble on top. The first one has been done to get you floating: 5 + 9 = 14.

H 15 5 10

I 19 7 12

J 5 5 25

M 2 11 13

K 2 9 18

L 12 2 6

N 32 4 8

O 8 18 26

P 6 5 30

Answer on page 48

HUNDRED HOP

Help Hilda hop across to any exit. Hilda can count only by 10s. She must hop across each number from 10 to 100 in order only once, and she can't cross back over her trail.

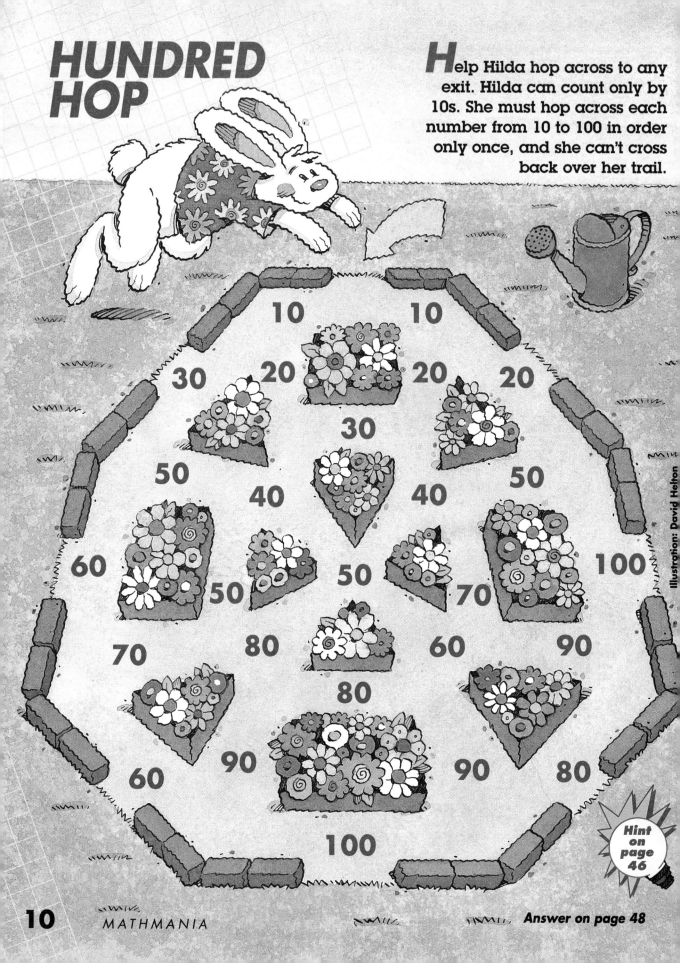

Illustration: David Helton

Hint on page 46

Answer on page 48

DOTS A LOT

First join the odd-numbered dots using one color. Then join the even-numbered dots using a different color to find a dancing beauty.

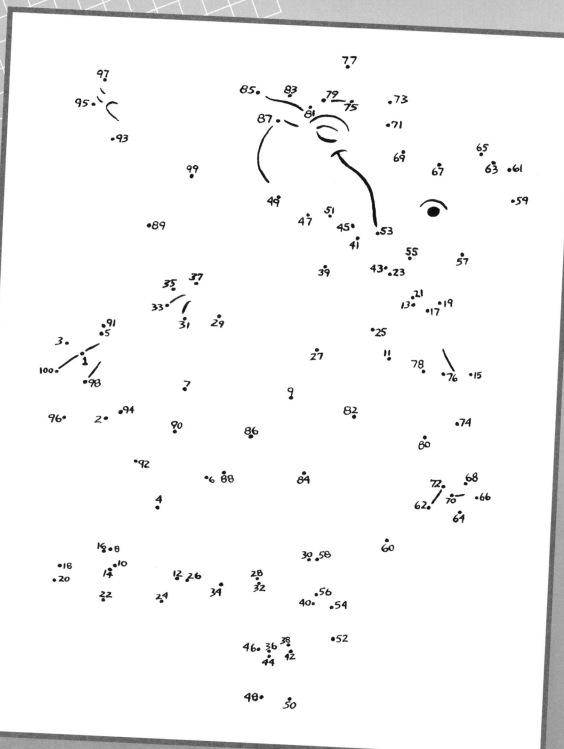

Illustration: Rob Sepanak

OFFICIAL INFORMATION

Each fact on the next page can be matched to one President below. To find the match, divide each fact's number in parentheses by 5. Match your answer to one of the numbers below the Presidents.

BILL CLINTON
14

CALVIN COOLIDGE
11

BENJAMIN HARRISON
8

ABRAHAM LINCOLN
15

ZACHARY TAYLOR
43

WM. HENRY HARRISON
31

JAMES MONROE
12

THEODORE ROOSEVELT
21

ANDREW JACKSON
18

JOHN QUINCY ADAMS
13

GERALD FORD
23

FRANKLIN D. ROOSEVELT
17

Answer on page 49

A. He and his wife were afraid of electricity and had their servants turn the lights on and off in the White House, rather than doing it themselves. (40)

B. He once played the saxophone on MTV. (70)

C. He thought football was too violent and wanted to ban the game. (105)

D. He was the fifth President and obtained Florida from Spain. (60)

E. His wife spun silk from silkworms on the mulberry trees that he had planted on the White House grounds. (65)

F. He once inherited $1,500 from his grandfather in Ireland. He lost all of it within a week. (90)

G. His father signed the Declaration of Independence, and his grandson was the twenty-third President. (155)

H. President James Madison and General Robert E. Lee were his cousins. (215)

I. He grew his whiskers on the advice of an eleven-year-old girl who wrote him and said he would look better with a beard. (75)

J. He kept a pet raccoon in the White House. (55)

K. While attending Yale University, he worked as a model and appeared in seventeen photos in *Look* magazine. (115)

L. He had polio and walked using braces and a cane. (85)

Illustration: Rick Geary

Hint on page 46

BLOCK PARTY

Can you tell which set
of blocks was used to
make each tower?

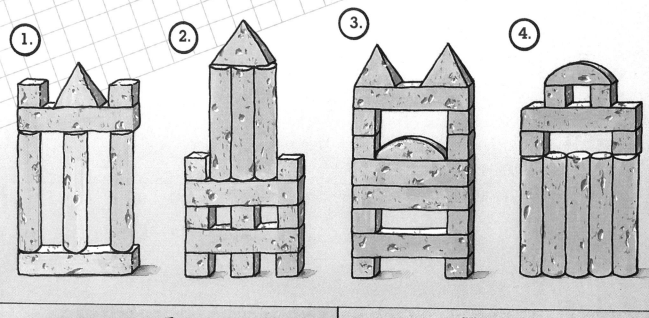

1.

2.

3.

4.

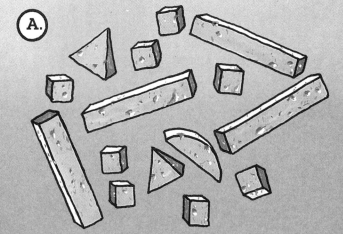

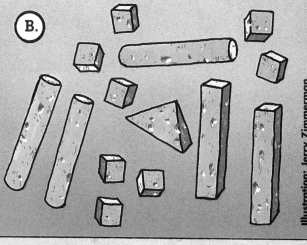

A.

B.

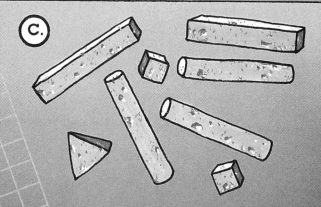

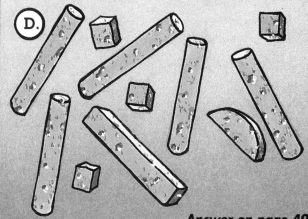

C.

D.

Illustration: Jerry Zimmerman

Answer on page 49

WAY TO GO

Read the six clues and fill in the blanks with the correct word. Under the letter of each word is a number. That number is also the answer to a math problem. Place the letters in the blanks that match the answers to the problems.

Illustration: Jim Paillot

1. Long series of cars pulled by a locomotive: ___ ___ ___ ___ ___
   1 2 3 4 5

2. Type of bull used to pull carts: ___ ___
   6 7

3. Two-wheeled ten-speed: ___ ___ ___ ___ ___ ___ ___
   8 4 9 10 9 11 12

4. Boat used to carry cars: ___ ___ ___ ___ ___
   13 12 2 2 10

5. Cowboy's transportation: ___ ___ ___ ___ ___
   14 6 2 15 12

6. Pioneers traveled west in this: ___ ___ ___ ___ ___
   16 3 17 6 5

Hint on page 46

What do you call lines of cabs in Dallas and Houston?

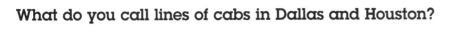

____ ____ ____   ____ ____ ____ ____ ____
2-1 7×2 5+7   6+4 13-1 10+1 11×1 12÷6 8×2

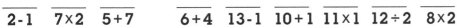

____ ____ ____ ____   ____ ____   ____ ____ ____ ____ ____.
8÷4 9-3 9+7 5×3   3×2 15-2   1×1 5-2 14÷2 3+1 9+6

LET'S LOOK IT UP

L ook at this index to help each person find the page needed for his or her topic.

Arnie wants to look up an article on his Adam's apple. He should turn to page ____.

Ramona requires reading regarding roller coasters. She should read page ____.

Edward wants to examine editorial epigrams on elephants. He should see page ____.

Frank is frantic to find facts about fog. These can be found on page ____.

Paula plans to peruse a piece on porcupines. The information she wants is on page ____.

Ted will take time to track down info on tides. He should target page ____.

Louise wants to look up lines about lizards. She should look on page ____.

Walter wants words of wisdom on windmills. He will do well on page ____.

INDEX

Answer on page 49

FRACTION FUN

To find the answer to our riddle, look for the letters in the circles. Each letter is in a section that equals a fraction of that circle. For example, the letter *U* is in a section that is $\frac{1}{3}$ the size of its circle. That means if you put 3 sections together, they would make a full circle. Find the right fraction, and write the letters in the matching spaces below. Then read down the column of letters to learn the answer to our riddle.

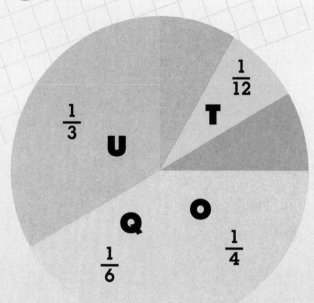

How much is the moon worth?

$\frac{1}{2}$	_____
$\frac{1}{4}$	_____
$\frac{1}{3}$	_____
$\frac{1}{8}$	_____
$\frac{1}{6}$	_____
$\frac{1}{3}$	_____
$\frac{1}{5}$	_____
$\frac{1}{8}$	_____
$\frac{1}{12}$	_____
$\frac{1}{10}$	_____
$\frac{1}{8}$	_____
$\frac{1}{16}$	_____

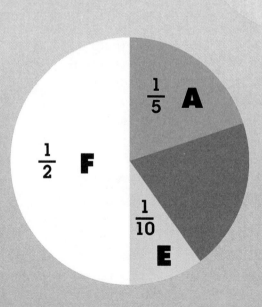

Hint on page 46

Answer on page 49

SKI SUMS

Add up the scores on the flags each skier passed to see who scored the most points on the slopes.

Illustration: Barbara Gray

CALLING CANADA

The numbers used here represent the numbers and letters on a telephone. For example, number 2 could stand for *A*, *B*, or *C*. It's up to you to punch in the right letters

Edmonton

Regina

Winnipeg

Answer on page 49

Hint on page 46

to decode the names of these Canadian cities, provinces, and territories. Remember, the same number can stand for different letters, even in the same word.

1. 329766
2. 688292
3. 734462
4. 2523782
5. 2254279
6. 6682746
7. 8676686
8. 33666866
9. 62648622
10. 66687325

11. 66673 529
12. 94664734
13. 727528666
14. 826268837
15. 2445549225
16. 6682 726842
17. 9448346773
18. 223346 475263
19. 63936863 5263
20. 727528243926

Illustration: John Nez

STACKING STANLEY

Stanley's aunt Nan finished carving these birds. Now he's trying to fit them into the blank area. Can you figure out the best way for Stan to place these carvings?

Hint on page 46

Answer on page 49

MINUS MAZE

You have 25 points as you enter this maze. You can get out only if you have exactly 0 points when you reach the exit. Choose the right path and subtract the amount the goblins want as you pass them.

ENTER

EXIT

10

12

0

Hint on page 47

5

3

11

8

13

26

6

13

1

14

30

9

2

1

27

2

19

29

5

12

4

14

22

Illustration: David Justice

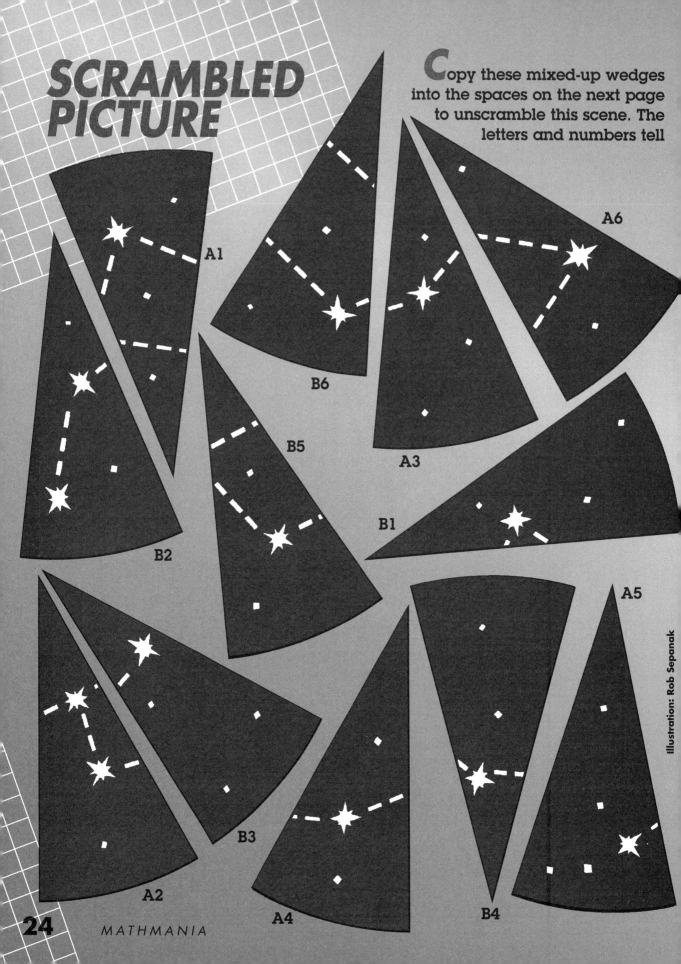

SCRAMBLED PICTURE

Copy these mixed-up wedges into the spaces on the next page to unscramble this scene. The letters and numbers tell

A1

A6

B6

B5

A3

B2

B1

A5

B3

A2

A4

B4

Illustration: Rob Sepanak

24   *MATHMANIA*

you where each wedge
belongs. The first one, A3,
has been done for you.

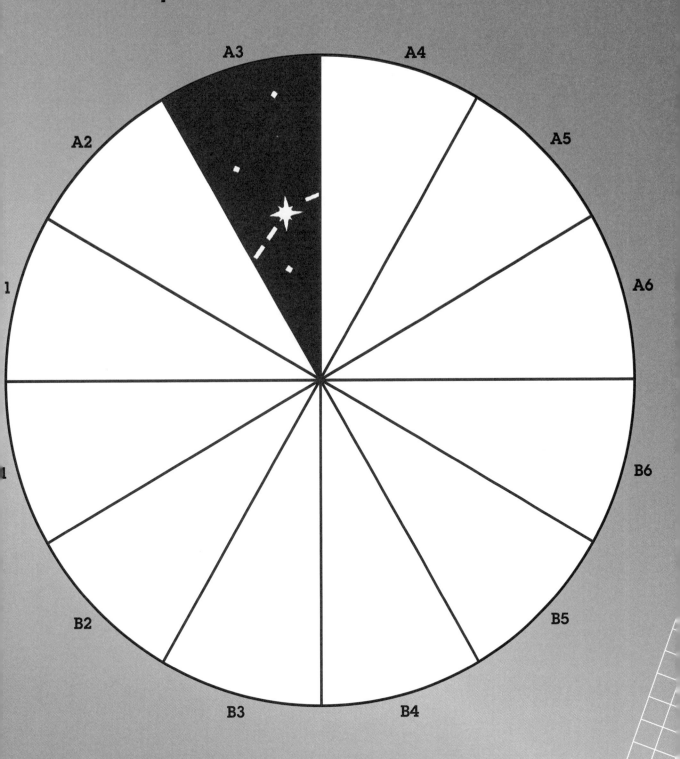

DIGIT DOES IT

Hattie Haystacks, the pin professional, has done it again. She's disrupted another pincushion convention by

Answer on page 50

nimbly placing thimbles into the proceedings. Hattie left a coded message for that super sleuth, Inspector Digit.

$\overline{11}\ \overline{7}\ \overline{21}\ \overline{14}$ $\overline{4}\ \overline{5}\ \overline{10}\ \overline{18}\ \overline{7}\ \overline{15}\ \overline{6}\ \overline{2}\ \overline{14}$ $\overline{11}\ \overline{4}\ \overline{12}\ \overline{4}\ \overline{6}$,

$\overline{20}\ \overline{2}\ \overline{3}$ $\overline{15}\ \overline{21}\ \overline{5}\ \overline{6}$ $\overline{18}\ \overline{4}\ \overline{5}$ $\overline{21}$

$\overline{6}\ \overline{8}\ \overline{4}\ \overline{5}\ \overline{12}$ $\overline{2}\ \overline{5}$ $\overline{9}\ \overline{7}$ $\overline{1}\ \overline{3}\ \overline{10}\ \overline{6}$.

$\overline{6}\ \overline{2}$ $\overline{5}\ \overline{7}\ \overline{7}\ \overline{11}\ \overline{13}\ \overline{7}$ $\overline{20}\ \overline{2}\ \overline{3}$, $\overline{4}$ $\overline{13}\ \overline{7}\ \overline{16}\ \overline{6}$

$\overline{J}\ \overline{M}$ $\overline{6}\ \overline{8}\ \overline{4}\ \overline{9}\ \overline{22}\ \overline{13}\ \overline{7}\ \overline{10}$ $\overline{22}\ \overline{7}\ \overline{8}\ \overline{4}\ \overline{5}\ \overline{11}$.

$\overline{4}\ \overline{16}$ $\overline{20}\ \overline{2}\ \overline{3}$ $\overline{10}\ \overline{6}\ \overline{4}\ \overline{15}\ \overline{17}$ $\overline{19}\ \overline{4}\ \overline{6}\ \overline{8}$ $\overline{4}\ \overline{6}$,

$\overline{20}\ \overline{2}\ \overline{3}$ $\overline{9}\ \overline{4}\ \overline{12}\ \overline{8}\ \overline{6}$ $\overline{12}\ \overline{7}\ \overline{6}$ $\overline{6}\ \overline{8}\ \overline{7}$

$\overline{18}\ \overline{2}\ \overline{4}\ \overline{5}\ \overline{6}$. $\overline{10}\ \overline{7}\ \overline{19}$ $\overline{13}\ \overline{2}\ \overline{5}\ \overline{12}$!

$\overline{8}\ .\ \overline{8}$.

Hint on page 47

Illustration: John Nez

MATHMAGIC

This trick will provide an amazing effect!

Lay some dominoes on a table. Let your friend choose one without telling you which one it is.

Your friend should multiply either of the two numbers on the domino by 5.

Now have your friend add 3 to that total.

Next, double the new total, and then add in the number from the other side of the domino.

Ask your friend to tell you his or her new total.

With a little concentration and some subtraction, you should be able to point directly to the chosen domino.

Illustration: Marc Nadel

BUZZ ABOUT

Buzz and Honey studied bees for a school project. They wanted to count the number of bees in a certain hive. One morning, Buzz sat by the hive and took notes. Later, he went home and gave Honey the clues below. She listened carefully and was able to figure out the answer. Can you do the same?

Half of the hive flew to the daffodil patch.

Of those remaining, one small bee stayed around the hive.

One-third of the remaining bees flew down to the peonies.

The other six bees flew to the lilac bushes.

How many bees did Buzz count in all?

Hint on page 47

Answer on page 50

MAIL CALL

Karen is in charge of this mail room. She has a very unique way of remembering which mail goes into what slots. Can you follow her list to put the correct

A goes in the first box (from the left) of the first row (at the top).

B goes in the second box of the second row.

C belongs in the fourth box of the fifth row.

D gets the fourth box down in the second column.

E goes between B and D to spell a word.

F goes in the upper right corner.

G belongs in the fourth box of the second row.

H goes in the fourth box of the third column.

I goes in the center box of the first row.

J goes at the bottom of the second column.

K goes in the first box of the last row.

L fits between I and F.

M is beside H and above C.

N is between B and G.

O goes beside G to spell a word.

P and Q share the center box.

R is in the center of the last column.

S is in the last box of the last row.

T comes between R and S to complete a word in that column.

U goes in the last remaining spot of the first row.

V will complete the bottom row.

W finishes off the fourth column.

X, Y, and Z go in the first column in order, starting with X in the fourth row.

Illustration: Scott Peck

Answer on page 50

TO: K. Bucki

letter on each box? Her rows go across and her columns go from top to bottom and left to right.

Now, to find the answer to Karen's favorite riddle, look at the box numbers. Match the letters in each box with the numbers beneath the blanks.

Why didn't the stamp go out last Saturday night?

‗‗ ‗‗ ‗‗ ‗‗ ‗‗ ‗‗ ‗‗ ‗‗ ‗‗ ‗‗
18 12 15   17 1 20 12   14 1 25

‗‗ ‗‗ ‗‗ ‗‗ ‗‗ ‗‗ ‗‗ ‗‗.
24 1   8   24 12 4 12 17

SAND ART

Can you draw this fish without crossing over or going back along any lines?

Illustration: Barbara Gray

Answer on page 50

SAVING UP

At the beginning of the year, Nick opened a savings account at the bank. Read the facts below to see if you can tell how much he has at year's end.

Every month of the past year, Nick earned $62.00 for doing yard and lawn work in his neighborhood. He put half of this into his account.

On his birthday, Nick's grandparents sent him $25.00. This went into the account.

In July, Nick needed a new mower for his lawn service. After selling his old mower for $30.00, he bought a new mower for $140.00. He took the difference out of his account.

Nick earned $16.22 in interest from the bank. This was credited to his account at the end of the year.

$62.00 a month ÷ 2

$140.00 $25.00

Interest $16.22

$30.00

What is Nick's total?

Hint on page 47

ABACUS ADDITION

An abacus is an ancient tool from Asia used to work mathematical problems. It is still in use today in some countries. The top bead in any column equals 5 when

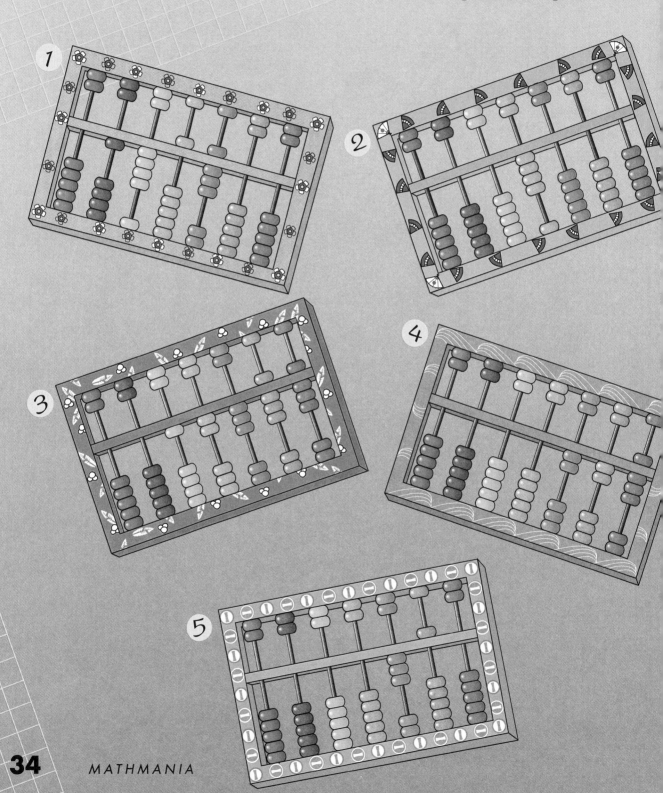

pushed down. Each bottom bead equals 1 when pushed up. The first column on the right is the ones place. The second column is the tens place, and so on.

For example: This would be 26.

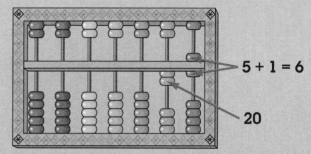

5 + 1 = 6

20

6

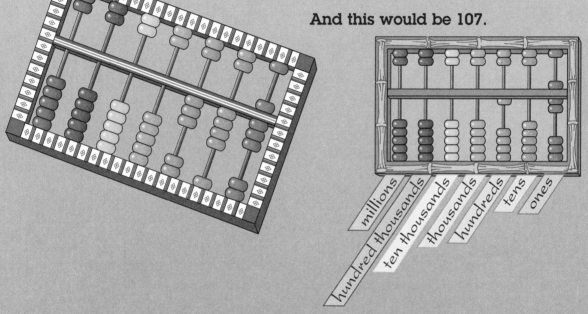

And this would be 107.

millions
hundred thousands
ten thousands
thousands
hundreds
tens
ones

You'll find some interesting facts about the Asian country of Japan if you can write in the number for each abacus shown.

1. Japan is _____ square miles.

2. Approximately _____ islands are included in all of Japan.

3. Japan's highest mountain, Mount Fuji, is _____ feet high.

4. The longest river is the Shinano-gawa, which is _____ miles long.

5. Sumo wrestlers can weigh up to _____ pounds.

6. The tallest lighthouse in the world is in Yokohama. It stands _____ feet high.

Illustration: Vilma Ortiz-Dillon

Answer on page 50

MATHMANIA

COMPASS COMEDY

Start at the circle that marks the northern point. Move in the directions given below. Write the letters you land on into the blanks. When you're done, read down the column of letters to find the answer to this riddle: **Where do bulls and cows go to dance?**

1. S 1 ___
2. SW 2 ___
3. SE 1 ___
4. E 3 ___
5. NW 2 ___
6. E 1 ___
7. NW 1 ___
8. W 2 ___
9. S 4 ___
10. E 2 ___
11. NE 2 ___

Illustration: R. Michael Palan

Hint on page 47

Answer on page 50

COLOR BY NUMBERS

Use the key to color in the shapes with the matching number of dots.

1 dot — Black	3 dots — Dark Blue
2 dots — White	4 dots — Light Blue
5 dots — Red	

Illustration: Rob Sepanak

Answer on page 50

NUMBER SEARCH

The answers to these 21 equations are hidden in the grid. The answers are spelled across, down, backward, or diagonally. Once you solve all the equations, search out the

1. 20 ÷ 2 = ___
2. 40 × 2 = ___
3. 22 - 18 = ___
4. 15 × 2 = ___
5. 40 ÷ 8 = ___
6. 42 + 12 = ___
7. 16 ÷ 8 = ___
8. 108 - 96 = ___
9. 11 + 7 = ___
10. 32 - 24 = ___
11. 36 + 27 = ___

12. 44 - 38 = ___
13. 28 × 2 = ___
14. 12 + 40 = ___
15. 45 ÷ 5 = ___
16. 39 - 16 = ___
17. 12 × 7 = ___
18. 83 - 52 = ___
19. 34 ÷ 2 = ___
20. 50 - 39 = ___
21. 6 ÷ 6 = ___

Illustration: Jim Paillot

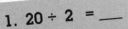

answers. When you find them all, read the leftover letters from top to bottom, going left to right on each new row, to find a riddle and its answer.

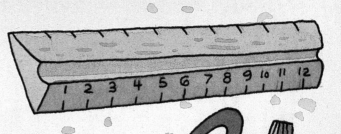

```
F I F T Y F O U R W H Y E
E D O O E I G H T Y M L A
T V H W E F M T A T E I E
E S I C T T I A W V N E I
E I S F W Y E E E E R S G
N X G A E S T N R H L E H
O T F H U I N F T W O V T
Y Y N Y T X G Y I S H E E
T T O E S Y T H ? F T N E
R H R H S N F E T Y O T N
I R H I E A F O U R V E I
H E X W H E S Q U U A E N
T E T R E T F E E R T N !
```

Answer on page 51

LIBRARY LAUGHS

Dewey has some funny books in his library. To check one out, you've got to solve each equation. Then go to the shelves to find the volume with the number that matches each answer. Put the matching letter in the blank beside each answer. Read down the letters you've filled in to find the title and author of the book Dewey just finished reading.

$8 + 7 =$ _____ _____
$14 - 2 =$ _____ _____
$2 \times 2 =$ _____ _____
$18 \div 3 =$ _____ _____
$15 + 6 =$ _____ _____
$21 - 3 =$ _____ _____
$7 \times 2 =$ _____ _____
$9 \div 1 =$ _____ _____
$14 + 6 =$ _____ _____
$25 - 4 =$ _____ _____
$3 \times 6 =$ _____ _____
$20 \div 4 =$ _____ _____
$8 - 6 =$ _____ _____
$5 \times 5 =$ _____ _____
$9 \div 9 =$ _____ _____
$9 + 5 =$ _____ _____
$16 - 2 =$ _____ _____
$4 \times 5 =$ _____ _____
$30 \div 6 =$ _____ _____
$2 + 3 =$ _____ _____
$14 - 3 =$ _____ _____

Illustration: Scott Peck

Answer on page 51

Hint on page 47

DIAMOND DOME

This is a blueprint of the Diamond Dome development. Right now, only six spaces are set aside for house lots. The developer wants to put in six more lots, but he can only afford to add three more roads. Can you help change the blueprint by adding three straight roads to make twelve equal-sized lots in all?

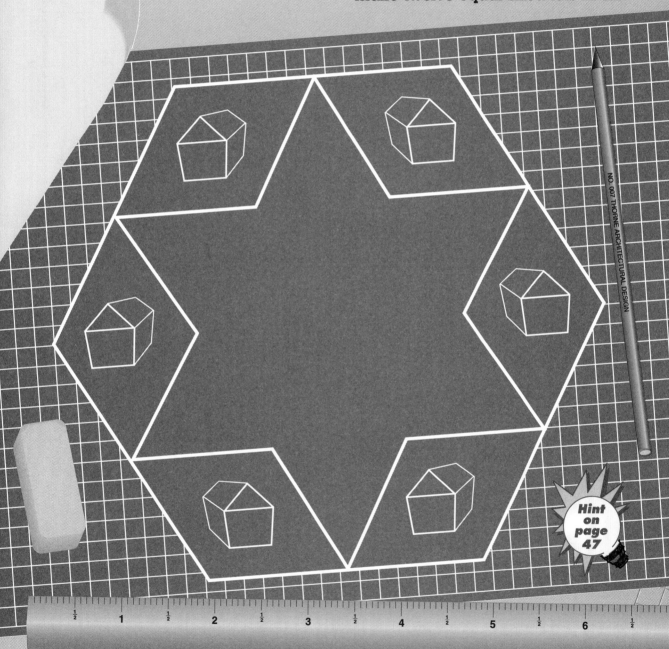

Hint on page 47

Answer on page 51

SHOW TIMES

Fred of the Forest
Run Time: 1:50
Show Times:
1:00   3:00   5:00   7:00   9:00

The Wizard of Ogs
Run Time: 2:15
Show Times:
12:30   3:00   5:30   8:00   10:30

Gojira
Run Time: 2:20
Show Times:
12:15   2:50   5:15   7:45   10:10

Planet of the Moops
Run Time: 2:10
Show Times:
12:00   2:15   4:40   7:00   9:30

Tall Marines
Run Time: 1:45
Show Times:
12:45   2:45   4:45   6:45   8:45

TICKETS

NOW PLAYING

Jerry loves the movies but can't go that often. When he finally gets a chance, he likes to see as many movies as possible. He wants to buy five tickets to watch all the movies at this theater in one day. He also wants a schedule that will leave him with the least amount of time between the end of one movie and the beginning of the next. Can you read the times to arrange Jerry's schedule?

Hint on page 47

Answer on page 51

SHOW TIMES II

Julie and Jon met Jerry in time to see one movie. Read through their schedules for the day to see when they were able to get there. Can you tell what time each arrived, who got there first, and which movie they watched with Jerry?

Julie's schedule —
Got up at 8:05 a.m. Took a long shower for 20 minutes, then spent 35 minutes getting dressed. Took Spot for a quarter-hour walk. Spot broke loose to chase a squirrel. Took 15 minutes to get him back. Fed Spot and had breakfast myself, which took 45 minutes. Walked to the library to return books, 25 minutes each way. Vacuumed living room and upstairs for 40 minutes. Fixed clogged vacuum hose — took an extra 5 minutes. Read a book for 30 minutes. Watched news program for half an hour, then watched *Captain Colossal* for 10 minutes. Popped down to the market for milk and bread, 20 minutes. Took Spot to the park for a run, 50 minutes. Stopped for ice cream, quarter hour. Walked to movies in 15 minutes. Arrived at:

Jon's schedule —
Woke at 8:25. Waited 5 minutes for hot water. Took bath and got dressed in 45 minutes. Couldn't find matching socks, needed extra 5 minutes. Made phone call to Mom, another 45 minutes. Ran to park and jogged around twice, 50 minutes. Stopped by cafe for breakfast on way home, 40 minutes. Bought the newspaper and checked out some new magazines, 10 minutes. Chatted with neighbor, quarter hour. Watched game show, half hour. Went to bank, 25 minutes each way. At home, waited for hot water for another 5 minutes, then showered for 10 minutes. Took a nap for 55 minutes. Walked to movies in 5 minutes. Arrived at:

Answer on page 51

Illustration: Rocky Fuller

MEASURE MATCH

Numerical measurements are everywhere. Many of them are abbreviated. Match each measurement here to the object it measures.

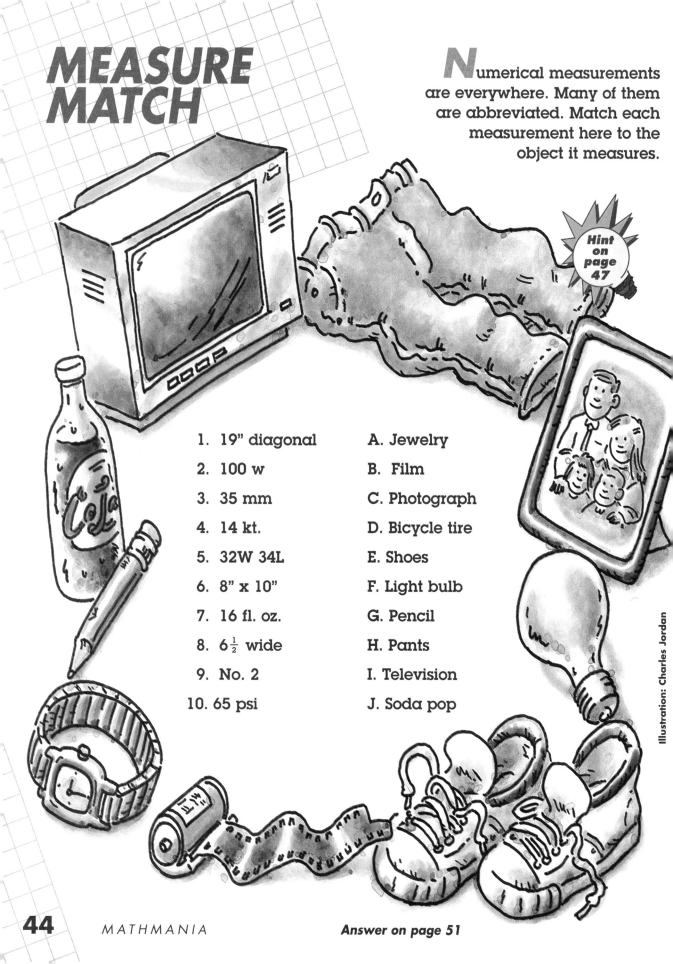

Hint on page 47

1. 19" diagonal
2. 100 w
3. 35 mm
4. 14 kt.
5. 32W 34L
6. 8" x 10"
7. 16 fl. oz.
8. $6\frac{1}{2}$ wide
9. No. 2
10. 65 psi

A. Jewelry
B. Film
C. Photograph
D. Bicycle tire
E. Shoes
F. Light bulb
G. Pencil
H. Pants
I. Television
J. Soda pop

Illustration: Charles Jordan

Answer on page 51

NUMBER PLEXERS

Our computer is printing out strings of numbers, all with different answers. Can you follow the instructions for each string to make sense of it all? The numbers will not change position, though they may be grouped together differently in each case. All problems must be worked from left to right.

1. 6 5 4 3 2 1 = 975
Place one addition symbol to get 975.

2. 6 5 4 3 2 1 = 333
Place one subtraction symbol to get 333.

3. 6 5 4 3 2 1 = 636
Place one addition symbol and one subtraction symbol to get 636.

4. 6 5 4 3 2 1 = 43
Place one subtraction symbol and one addition symbol to get 43.

5. 6 5 4 3 2 1 = 38
Place two addition symbols and one subtraction symbol to get 38.

6. 6 5 4 3 2 1 = 52
Place one multiplication symbol, one addition symbol, and one subtraction symbol to get 52.

Answer on page 51

Illustration: Scott Peck

Hint on page 47

HINTS AND BRIGHT IDEAS

*T*hese hints may help with some of the trickier puzzles.

SHE LOVES ME (page 6)

When you add the petals in the first flower, your total is 20. The number in the center is 17. Since 20 − 17 = 3, pluck off any petal with a 3 on it.

TALLEST OF ALL (page 7)

There are 12 inches in 1 foot. Divide 12 into the inches given to convert the number into feet. Then add the foot total to the number of feet already given. The remainder is the leftover inches.

HUNDRED HOP (page 10)

The numbers Hilda will hop to are 10, 20, 30, 40, 50, 60, 70, 80, 90, and 100 in that order.

OFFICIAL INFORMATION (pages 12-13)

To divide by 5, remember this: If the number ends in 0, double all the numbers before the 0. For example, let's divide 20 by 5. Double the 2 in 20 to get 4 — 20 ÷ 5 = 4. If the number you're dividing ends in 5, double the numbers before the 5 and then add 1.

WAY TO GO (page 15)

Blanks with similar numbers get the same letter.

FRACTION FUN (page 18)

One-half is the largest area of any circle given, while $\frac{1}{16}$ is the smallest. One-half is *F*, and $\frac{1}{16}$ is *S*.

CALLING CANADA (pages 20-21)

The words are listed in alphabetical order based on word size. Moose Jaw and Chilliwack are just two of the places we called.

STACKING STANLEY (page 22)

Birds can be moved upside down or around to fit next to one another.

MINUS MAZE (page 23)
The first two numbers you come to are 3 and 6.

DIGIT DOES IT (pages 26-27)
The word *Inspector* appears in the note's greeting. Use the coded numbers in this word to help figure out the rest of the message.

BUZZ ABOUT (page 29)
Three bees flew to the peonies. Try adding the last three clues together. That number should be half your total.

SAVING UP (page 33)
To begin Nick's calculations, multiply $31 times 12 months in a year.

COMPASS COMEDY (page 36)
Directions with two letters, like NW or SW, mean that you should move in a diagonal direction. NW is northwest, so you'd want to move toward the corner where north and west meet.

LIBRARY LAUGHS (page 40)
Remember to consult the books to find the letter that matches each number.

DIAMOND DOME (page 41)
The three roads you must add will cross in the center of the blueprint.

SHOW TIMES (page 42)
Jerry will look for a schedule that keeps the movies close. He doesn't want to sit around too long between films.

MEASURE MATCH (page 44)
The abbreviation *mm* stands for "millimeter" and is a measure of film.

NUMBER PLEXERS (page 45)
Numbers will form different combinations. For example, the numbers could be 654 + 3 - 21, or they could be 6 - 54 + 3 - 21. One of the two choices here is the answer to the third question.

ANSWERS

SHE LOVES ME (page 6)
17 flower: remove a 3 petal
22 flower: remove a 2 petal
31 flower: remove the 5 petal
25 flower: remove a 5 petal
34 flower: remove the 2 petal
18 flower: remove the 6 petal

TALLEST OF ALL (page 7)
Ally—18 feet 6 inches
Bozz—17 feet 8 inches
Cosmo—16 feet 6 inches
Denali—16 feet 4 inches
Elsa—18 feet 8 inches. Elsa is the tallest.

BUBBLE BUDDIES (pages 8-9)
A. $5 + 9 = 14$
B. $7 + 16 = 23$
C. $21 ÷ 7 = 3$
D. $27 ÷ 3 = 9$
E. $33 - 11 = 22$
F. $3 × 4 = 12$
G. $28 - 4 = 24$
H. $15 - 5 = 10$
I. $19 - 7 = 12$
J. $5 × 5 = 25$
K. $2 × 9 = 18$
L. $12 ÷ 2 = 6$
M. $2 + 11 = 13$
N. $32 ÷ 4 = 8$
O. $8 + 18 = 26$
P. $6 × 5 = 30$

HUNDRED HOP (page 10)

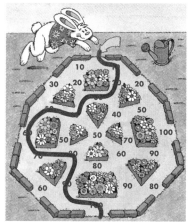

DOTS A LOT (page 11)

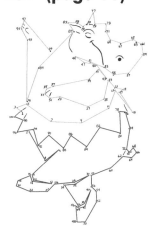

COVER
Muscles: $14 × 34 = 476$
Hercules: $317 + 179 = 496$
Moose: $987 - 483 = 504$

MUST COME DOWN (page 3)

$24 + 13 = 37$ (Odd) $19 - 3 = 16$ (Even)
$33 + 23 = 56$ (Even) $45 - 24 = 21$ (Odd)
$25 + 21 = 46$ (Even) $57 - 25 = 32$ (Even)
$12 + 26 = 38$ (Even) $28 - 13 = 15$ (Odd)
$57 + 22 = 79$ (Odd) $49 - 36 = 13$ (Odd)

COWBOY CASH (pages 4-5)
A.	Bandanna	$.10
B.	Lasso	$7.75
C.	Rain slicker	$2.75
D.	Cotton shirt	$1.25
E.	Blanket	$.30
F.	Spurs	$.70
G.	Saddle	$40.00
H.	Stetson hat	$10.00
I.	Leather boots	$20.00
	TOTAL	$82.85

OFFICIAL INFORMATION (pages 12-13)

A. Benjamin Harrison $(40 \div 5 = 8)$
B. Bill Clinton $(70 \div 5 = 14)$
C. Theodore Roosevelt $(105 \div 5 = 21)$
D. James Monroe $(60 \div 5 = 12)$
E. John Quincy Adams $(65 \div 5 = 13)$
F. Andrew Jackson $(90 \div 5 = 18)$
G. William Henry Harrison $(155 \div 5 = 31)$
H. Zachary Taylor $(215 \div 5 = 43)$
I. Abraham Lincoln $(75 \div 5 = 15)$
J. Calvin Coolidge $(55 \div 5 = 11)$
K. Gerald Ford $(115 \div 5 = 23)$
L. Franklin Delano Roosevelt $(85 \div 5 = 17)$

BLOCK PARTY (page 14)

A. 3   B. 2   C. 1   D. 4

WAY TO GO (page 15)

1. train   4. ferry
2. ox   5. horse
3. bicycle   6. wagon

What do you call lines of cabs in Dallas and Houston?
THE YELLOW ROWS OF TAXIS

LET'S LOOK IT UP (pages 16-17)

Arnie—page 146   Paula—page 61
Ramona—page 114   Ted—page 233
Edward—page 44   Louise—page 60
Frank—page 170   Walter—page 188

FRACTION FUN (page 18)

How much is the moon worth?
FOUR QUARTERS

SKI SUMS (page 19)

Jai—$5 + 3 + 6 + 8 + 1 = 23$
Mari—$7 + 8 + 2 + 1 + 2 = 20$
Kim—$2 + 9 + 4 + 4 + 3 = 22$
Sven—$5 + 6 + 5 + 4 + 1 = 21$
Jai scored the most points.

CALLING CANADA (pages 20-21)

1. DAWSON   11. MOOSE JAW
2. OTTAWA   12. WINNIPEG
3. REGINA   13. SASKATOON
4. ALBERTA   14. VANCOUVER
5. CALGARY   15. CHILLIWACK
6. ONTARIO   16. NOVA SCOTIA
7. TORONTO   17. WHITEHORSE
8. EDMONTON   18. BAFFIN ISLAND
9. MANITOBA   19. NEWFOUNDLAND
10. MONTREAL   20. SASKATCHEWAN

STACKING STANLEY (page 22)

MINUS MAZE (page 23)

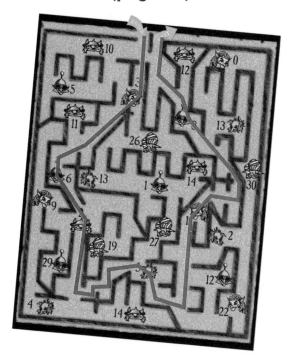

SCRAMBLED PICTURE (pages 24-25)

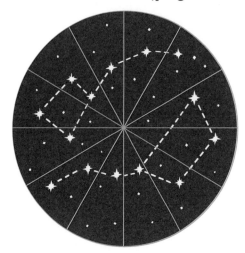

DIGIT DOES IT (pages 26-27)

Dear Inspector Digit,

You can't pin a thing on me. Just to needle you, I left 19 thimbles behind. If you stick with it, you might get the point. Sew long! H.H.

a–21	g–12	m–9	t–6
b–22	h–8	n–5	u–3
c–15	i–4	o–2	w–19
d–11	j–1	p–18	y–20
e–7	k–17	r–14	
f–16	l–13	s–10	

MATHMAGIC (page 28)

Subtract 6 from whatever total your friend says. This should leave you with a two-digit number. Those two numbers are the numbers on the originally chosen domino. For instance, 26 would be: [domino]. If you get a one-digit number when you subtract 6, that means one side of the original tile is blank.

BUZZ ABOUT (page 29)

Buzz counted 20 bees.

MAIL CALL (pages 30-31)

A	U	I	L	F
Z	B	N	G	O
Y	E	P/Q	W	R
X	D	H	M	T
K	J	V	C	S

Why didn't the stamp go out last Saturday night?
HER DATE WAS CANCELED.

SAND ART (page 32)

SAVING UP (page 33)

$31.00 × 12 months =	$372.00
Birthday	$25.00
Interest	$16.22
TOTAL	$413.22
Money for mower	–$110.00
FINAL TOTAL	$303.22

ABACUS ADDITION (pages 34-35)

1. 145,800 square miles
2. 4,000 islands
3. 12,388 feet high
4. 228 miles long
5. 350 pounds
6. 348 feet high

COMPASS COMEDY (page 36)

Where do bulls and cows go to dance?
TO A MEATBALL

COLOR BY NUMBERS (page 37)